IT HURT, BUT I'M ALIVE

IT HURT, BUT I'M ALIVE

STEVE MONTEROSSO

Monty Writes

Dedicated to my family and friends. Thank you for always supporting
me and pushing me forward.

Gauze

Get discovered, get distracted, get disowned
Busy hearts
Feeling more like trinkets
Than actual weapons
We had a rare season of smiles
Falling from the trees
Like the leaves
Brown, red, yellow, orange
And some of them were still green
We had the storm circle back
And cover up our eyes
We could feel the clouds floating
Chilling our spines
We don't need this feeling now
Growling stomachs
Laying on the couch
Fire on the throats and backs
Using pocket knives
To pick the dirt out of our nails
Rolled up sleeves
Is this work or is this jail?
Get recovered, get recycled, get renowned

902

Song machines trying to give us repair
Repentance in a dazed stare
Squeezing from fruit for a juice that never comes
Dried out from previous beats of the drums
Rolling platforms and rolling blackouts
Somehow the world keeps spinning on doubts
Moving muscles on memory
Justifiably trying different sets of keys
Getting sick from this playground equipment
Spitting up since it kept spinning around
The wind tearing your voice to shreds
Bringing a fever to the sound
Bitter but better bass line
Caked in equal parts sweat and regret
Steering wheel scorched into the concrete
Crystal clear cut teeth all divvied up from a careless bet
Reborn and re-forged in the backwash and backdraft
Some schematics etched out
Separately on a napkin and a notepad
There's already dirt and dead skin
Scuffing up a new pair of glasses
Unable to see the piano keys
An out of tune tidal wave passes
Blistering all of our feet

Squeeze
This fiction made the oil paintings scream
Dripping like watercolors and drying instantly
Exiting northwest when I'm still awake
Batteries low while gambling at high stakes
And I just kept pricking my finger
Too afraid to even listen to the music
Too afraid to move knick-knacks away from danger
That were too close to the shelf's edge
Navigating the water in a passive approach
As I land, I watch caves catch fire
Stalagmites becoming candles and torches
Not really lighting the way
And that's something I admire
Just weaving the crowd through entertainment
Getting sleeping sheep ready for an alarm
They appreciated the warnings
Only some signs of long lasting harm
Watching others squish seasons
Between their fingers
In the palms of another hand
They somehow safely fill the gap
Even though it's just pretend
Another space for rent to disguise distance
Nodding off but just not enough
And it's different for most
Consumed by fidgeting and listlessness
They raise a glass and toast
To the sudden and hopefully brief loss

Of the comfort they had in leaving
Of the safety nets and sudden projects
That made us rummage through photo albums
But also sick to our stomachs
Golden gills trying to breathe in the thin air
Born and bred in this smoke and smog
It somehow helped my roots
And it's going to keep being a slog
Wind scars and scores a burn on the skin
My own fault that I couldn't starve in the distance
I'm nodding off but just not enough

Every Opportunity
I'm repeating
And speaking in failures
Cartoon antics
Creating too much danger
Sorry to keep you waiting
It was safer
Deep in the dugout
But the derby took forever
I'd rather stay at home
With the dog
With the remote
While the batteries corrode
Is this enough
To pull you out of bed?
Stifled in the deep end
Sipping on silence
Even though ties were cut
It wasn't enough
Theme songs
In the background for too long
You woke up
Healthy dose of overcast
And slight sun in your mug
But the meal won't last
Spinning coins
Instead of tossing them
Not calling it in the air
Only during momentum

It's a new tenacity
For both you and me
But we're still tethered
Tarred and feathered
Platinum and dozing off
We couldn't control
Any of our coughs
They made us hysterical & nervous
We should stay up
Later than intended
Not a hefty price
For just a bit of happiness
You heard the ashes hiss
Mixing with the sand
Dragged by tide
As you had wished

Pressurize

First night nerves and collapsible coffee stains
I can't help but strain my brain
Green starry night on the ceiling gets deconstructed
Torn apart? No, the glue just wore off as luck would have it
I'm giving myself a hand so I won't drown
But I don't think this is going to help the result
It just all feels like a catapult
With all the weight on the ribs
I hear cracking and crunching
Realizing only fools wear crowns
And chains while pouncing
Letting words flow over their heads slowly and satirically
I let them burn their own bridges
Continuously fidgeting in my bed
While I still gasp for a decent pocket of fresh air
I thought someone would keep it clean
I'm just drawing on wood to pass the time
Gorging on kettle chips and cheap boxed wine
I'm sorry for being pessimistic about the fabric
Was just waiting for nothing
While watching my language
You just knew you couldn't cut it down
The moment of recovery that would surround
And fever dreams that left us out

Minute Hand
I'm just dragging
Mud and sand
In my shoes
Pebbles just tagging
Along for a ride
Knocked the tooth loose

My body was drained
The tripod tilted my brain
Held it in place
My whole frame
Split like wood
This isn't turning out good

We're still practicing
Trigger happy tug of war
I'm just face planting
And still being a good sport

But it's pretty easy to bleat
With the sounds of defeat
And to keep a laugh
In the conversations

Better than a lover's spat
That wouldn't go far
Would just be money
Piling up in a swear jar

It's a little uncommon
For me to be calm
But I was whistling
And left the light on

Fueled

I'll stay courteous and careful by the center
Hiding from you
While you hide and lie to yourself and others
Do you want to play the part of earth or water?
There are better parts to play
Than selfishness or stupidity
They're even worse when mixed
Try to stay in the bliss
I left myself inside a tornado
Needles in my ears and quills in my arms
I don't know who caused me harm
It makes a good maze
A peculiar puzzle that puts me in a daze
I might not survive in this form
Piloting a plastic ship in a glass bottle
Through a perfect paper storm
And even with these stipulations
I'd still sing to you in end

Wishing On
A star, to stay healthy
Dandelions, to feel young again
Candles, to be wealthy
Eyelashes, not to be nervous
11:11 on the VCR, to be strong
Asking ladybugs
That these requests don't take too long

Rated PG
Leaving the bike in the garage
Going on foot
One full lap around Pangea
Laughing through the montage
Falling in and not acting my age
A crack in the coliseum
The landing was fairly soft
Let's put some expectations of extinction on this
Or everyone will walk out of the theater
Unentertained and remiss
Eyes out in every direction
Watching a decade long day
I could use some camouflage
And a lot less attention
This all feels like a bad massage
That could break the neck
Swimming or swaying through the desert
The flailing through a frequency
I'm losing the happy tune I started with
Waking up in a cheap, tattered polo shirt
Did you see the planes
Flapping their wings?
It's like you could hear the engines sing
Chirping with the birds
That they're desperate to imitate
Feels like I lifted the whole world
When I woke up
Shoulders popping when I stretched

I guess when the treasure's found
I can pay for replacements
Maybe we all could use some new parts
I won't be cliched and ask for a new heart
Lungs would be better
This current pair
Has left me far behind others
So much so that I'm tuned out from tricks
And cheated out of fair tips
I couldn't even complete a fraction of a lap
I'm just winded as usual
And ready for a nap
I've been on the docks for ages
Hitchhiker thumb in the wrong direction
And a green thumb that seems proud
Of withered petals
And some slight discoloration
It's time for some sedation
Until we all get back to the castle
Here's to hoping
You enjoyed the moving pictures
And learned a lesson

Staccato

I'll never see a cent for this
Unnerving questions and faux bliss
It's come down to warriors vs. lawyers
That's all that's left standing when the dirt slept
Some want blood
Others want money
Most of them want both
Meanwhile, you wanted us to sway in the silk
To ignore the commotion and guilt
Yet kept crying about the spills
Pat yourself on the back
For doing the bare minimum in friendship
Poorly calculated, misplaced aggression
There seems to be a new king and queen in every scene
And wannabe warlocks and witches
Trying to dethrone them and take the keys
The hypocrisy is oddly tasty
I'm sure that went unnoticed as well
It's an interesting head swell
Celebrate by the sink
Spray paint on the lips and teeth
Scenery and still life
Dancing around debt and dust
Caving in with the coffee cup
Getting a kick to the elbow then the ribs
And paintball bruises on the back
At least I wore a face mask

Discombobulated
A few books
In the foreground
And the background
Got a buckshot
Damn, this stinks
Gunpowder makes
The nostrils sting
Sulfur in the soup
This route in a constant loop
Sorry to be profane
But fuck this carpool
I'm leaving to go get drunk
I thought exchanging gifts
Might be sort of fun
They say it's all in the meditation
The micromanagement
Mismatched by miscreants
I hope the rings
Never fit
A fake love that will stew
That will sit
The glued eyes
Are just fine
They sit well with the things I need
A raspy voice ricocheting
Off the necklace chain and beads
There are still some people
Trying to lick their plates clean

Lean in on the trends
Cassette tapes
And graffiti on the skin
Designs intricate, dark, & tedious
It's them vs. us
On a 2-disc set
Pirated and grainy
Watermarked and fuzzy
It's almost perfect

Flannel

Starting to outgrow
Blood spattered charcoal
Cowards rarely or never reply
And boast big budget goodbyes
But we never see a coin
Sink into the sand
You got what you needed
Bucket list bullet point cleared
Broad shoulders
And a blanket that's heated
Slick steps taken on the stairs
Face painting facial hair
Can't distinguish the baby speak
From the growling
It's unique
Only a casket for the mind
And one rose for the cheek
Smoke specifically for the eyes
Invested in causing a bigger leak
A few jewels left in the water
And moss overtaking the ladder
Still a few pencil shavings to consume
A rock cut in half to make a new room
Try not to track in dirt
Don't you dare track in mud
Whatever god help you
If I find a single crumb

Soot & Sugar
All I want
Is a little time to figure out
All we've lost
And how to get it back
Without reasonable doubt
It's not going well
It's like swimming through dirt
Being crushed by the earth's crust
It's a fresh yet familiar hell
The constructs are failing
With what I commissioned them to do
I'll humor this for a little while
Burn it down
Show my teeth
Bite it out and snarl
And I'd like to let my conscience realize
I have a lengthy laundry list
That will just complicate my life
"You've grown dull, darling."
They tell me
Yeah, I'm cool with that
Sitting on a footstool while at bat
An embarrassing blur sitting still
It's from a lack of feeling
Not boorish, stubborn iron will
Communication killed me
This time it wasn't curiosity
Steel wool against the folds

Of my brain and I burrow
And borrow until the days get cold
I just want to be comfortable while I sleep
And I found some comfort in our scenes
Now someone's setting off
Some bombs in the backroom
The blast was a little rough
But I'm still standing
Perpetually practicing
Unintentionally parading imperfections

Cough Syrup

Stage play on a stagecoach
3 inch cut on the lips
Delivering lines from a dry throat
"How did you bite your nails through gloves?"
With a nervous touch
But most importantly, with love
One lash after another to the back
Cutting cake to celebrate
Adding more bulge to the food baby
Everyone else is dancing around
With their teeth falling out
By their own hands or common nature
Paper tigers glued together
Still trying to impress fathers & mothers
With different shades in a meaningless parade
Taking place in a dying mall
Noise complaints from the bones in the wall
One headless statue in the hall
Secret stories and worthless bindings
Turn up the snow and sketchy lines
It's a white out, it's blinding
Insufficient funds and frozen blood
Some survived the flood
Others drowned in the mud
The engine has a case of rot gut
And I can't help but ask
Is what I lost enough?

Food for Birds

A vacant lot crowded with litter
A collection of old coins was spent
And I had never felt sicker
The cough moved in overnight
It got worse with the pain my throat
Tired and laying on my back in the sun
There's a fight between the vultures and the crows
Over who has the right to pick at me when I'm done
I've grown bored watching them
So I'll just shut my eyes for a little while
Woke up, no body, just bones are left
Somehow I still could see
Were the corpses of defeated crows
And the vultures
Poisoned by the meat from my bones
Boom went the pieces when I had an idea
Of how to get home on my current budget
My cup runneth over with a whole lot of nothing
Not a dime, not a nickel, not a cent
How the hell am I going to make this month's rent?
I asked while following the tumbleweeds
If I run I'll just collapse into a mess
Meanwhile I made a map in my head
Probably just a joke for now
To pass the time until the tendons
And sanity grow back
Desperate to have a cigar in the meantime
Since my humor is too dry and lowbrow

Finally on par with my dad's puns
Which reminded me
I have a bone to pick with him, just for fun
I finally found my way home
To avoid the landlord
I had to sneak through the window
It was hard getting to the second floor
With no joints or fingertips
I couldn't climb well without a good grip
Even though the muscle and fat were lost
At least I was rid of that bothersome cough

Cartoons
I'm sure you took a bigger bite
Of the faith and the bullets
In just one day
You conquered more
Than I did in a lifetime
It's not always easy
I'm not always like this
I left a spell somewhere
It's a fresh new hell
Burnt to a crisp in a waking nightmare
Logs tied to each leg
A cumbersome and clumsy
Outfit that I'm left to dread
Count to three
Or count to ten
Turn to page 213
We'll start from there
Instead of then
Just a little more color
Just a few more marbles
I need the truth
Negative or positive
And I'll need proof
Bigger trees bring bigger fees
Found myself
At a misty mountain base
Mind's playing tricks
And I'm hearing things

More and more anxious as a phone rings
Tag sale of all the gravel and rocks
I haven't made back a penny
Still in debt and down on luck
Kingdom made of sand
Crowns made of paper
Another sad sucker
Thirsting for the '90s
The nostalgia will go sooner or later
Stand as a prize winning pawn
Worthy of faint, far away applause
From broken hands and arms
A bunch of young lovers
Who think nothing of the shards
Of broken glass
And powerless knick-knacks
Not too concerned with
The candlewick
And hurried, messy magic
We left a few things unattended
It's better that way for a while

Think & Growl

Anger induced coin toss
Fingers crossed
We can finally become lost
Anchored to ankles
Syringes and cigarettes
Flesh and soul made of binary code
The running water woke us up
The outlets aren't a good mix with this
A nice prescription of science and silence
Different concerts going on in our heads
And shadow people taking up the whole bed
So much for this permanent stitch
We can feel the skin start to separate and itch
Shards of glass in the gums and jaw
Injured without insurance
Seeking mercy from stepparents
That's just what life is
Series of false pimples and blemishes
Someone hand me the remote
I miss my favorite TV tropes
Watch them spiral
In a stationary water bottle
I love everything about it
We began with so much steam
And a furrowed brow
Once open 24 hours
But we're closed now

Rat

You felt that way once
You had fun
Now tying a noose to a rock
Chewing pills and buying rolling papers
But we left out the tobacco
The impression of an inhaler
In the back of a blue jeans pocket
A few film frames in a locket
Brine, bile, and balloons
As well as string and beef stock for stew
You've seen and tasted it all before
Here's some hydrogen peroxide for the sores
Talkative flies waltzing in
Tracking prints across the carpet
Until they get sucked in by a fan
Osculating their head, thorax, and guts
I think you left a tag on the handle
Admit that you caught the chump change
Commoner with a lot of cash
Grasping at straws and clutching at pearls
I think I'm going to hurl

Ampersand
Penny down for deposit
Now to ask some foolish questions
Will you stay out?
Will you stick around?
Save what you can
But avoid the permanence
All my old friends stay drunk on the past
The glory days of a forgotten cast
Romantic comedies and dramedies
Using staples for a sad stability
Running naked through the road
Or drowning in the bathtub
Get your shoes off the goddamn coffee table
There's a reason there's a label
You want to get better
Lean forward and punch a pillow in anger
Pair of glasses below the bleachers
Drum set and gut feeling belonging to the teacher
Grey and white hairs used as currency
Keep stealing air from lungs
Like an 80's coming of age story
Covered in Summer and ingesting the Spring
Get used to the captain's boots
Standing in your way and kicking roots
Drinking ugly words
As they hunt forever
Through the ceiling
Through the basement

For fame and riches
From items others
Would call trash and rotten
That's when we ran out of road
The seatbelts came undone
The ribs were exposed
Cracked and split from everything
That we thought we should know

Visceral

Shoplift and shake it off
We shouldn't care about tonight
There's a better offer in this handshake
Than the one that blindsided you
From a coworker's rough draft
Steel bones in a different light
Dimples are starting to change
1:30 AM when I was voted out
I guess that was a good one
A good stroll where I was shot and put down
Slam dunks in the slaughterhouse
Plywood backboards
And trash can baskets
Pull out the sliver that piqued your interest
The meal is getting cold
The pets are getting tired
I wore them out for the day from fetch
Now curling the book binding
If I might be so bold
Cheap CGI tricks and pocket change failure
I still won't surrender

Insipid

Telling fibs through a loudspeaker
5 o'clock foreshadowing
Entrusted to the theater
Give me a bit of a hint
Or maybe a safety pin and splint
One second I'm full
The very next I'm hungry
But I'm just morbid and dull
And I can't thank you enough
Cotton swabs and a toothbrush
To clean up all this junk
Paper bag over my head
To hide the ugliness
While nature remodels the kitchen
Let's not lose any momentum
Sit out on the sidelines big guy
Everyone knows you've overstayed your welcome
You need a different vision

Settled
Alright, security....
What's it going to take to get you to leave?
Seems like the perfect night
To share excuses by candlelight
Mammoth memories being shared
Through a dinner without care
Finding one flaw after the other
Keeping our place with a dog ear to the paper
Drill into my forehead and let things spill out
Radiating a stupefied look in my self portrait
Headphones on and they cause a spark
It's a pissing contest in the dark
You stole all my lines and still needed to yell "cut"
It's too hot on the stage and I feel a rot in my gut
I should've rethought my major
Maybe things would've gone in our favor
Maybe they'd be completely different
It's only been 3 years of this
And I'm completely spent
I keep seeing you in those dreams
Waking up with a grunt or low pitched scream
I've got a mask on and a major facelift to the personality
Overhauled internal arguments
Where I can't win or leave
Just keep reading, just keep humming and ignoring
I'm accepting of this mess
And that I'll always be boring

Smoke & Love
How'd you feel about diamonds?
While I waded through the wallpaper
In the loudest silence
Subconsciously, you're sinking into the middle
But it's only a little

It got far too snug
In the smell of smoke and love
It's vacation time and we're failing the midterms
Spending the best days with soliloquies
Fizzled out with non sequiturs

Life's too short to be knocking on wood
Licking bones clean and circling
A mixture of a tremble and a shiver
Disposable recipes in the drink cupboard
They took all the credit
While you took all the pictures
And did all the work

You've been looking for a wallflower
One to dance with while you flounder
It's good to keep
A missing piece separate
And hum certain melodies

Crocodile tears and teeth
Leaving marks on the answering machine

I'm getting a little tired of shaking my bones
It's comical while watching myself turn to stone
Riding a bull all alone

I asked you to be careful
Of the boots and licorice
Books filled with comatose stones
Knowing one day they'll be capable
Of greatness and groans

We'll crush stems to dust for a scrapbook
Catalyst for little smiles and a new look
But maybe a little is enough
And new is just as important
It goes well with these imperfections

So what if I'm slouching
So what if I'm staggering
Through all the cutscenes
I'm not sure how else I should proceed

I won't use delusions
And I refuse to use excuses
While you proudly wear several hats
In your corner of the ring
Fighting off brats

You shouldn't care who's digging in
And certainly shouldn't care about
Those that are disapproving
They just linger on bad cravings and taste
Pretending their stares are loud

Torn tea bags make this a little too strong

Betraying and begging for enough
Nostrils still offended
By the strong scents of smoke and love
But maybe you'll start feeling better

Young Sketch

The sequence tried
To save some lives
I'm just parroting
All the pilots
With bum wings
And condescending responses
Quick cries and loud barks
For nicotine and alcohol
Say goodbye
To the point you grew
Rotting this time
In the living room
It happened so fast
But went on for so long
A modern blast
Of comedy that choked
All the life from the home
Uncommonly insensible
You bit the lip
Lit a cigarette
Green in the gills
Forgetting about the fresh air
Finding it on
The tip of your tongue
As well as the tip of the ocean
You decided to simply drain
And drink its contents

Dull Moment
It's a new shape of shame
Melting on the streets
Burning up and becoming lazy

Stuck in a lab
With classic epidemics
I have a feeling I'm problematic

No one's going to be agile
Lying on their back
With a gun to the elbow

Let me be clear
I don't care who's overseeing
It's time to for me to leave

I'll hold off
On emergency calls for now
I have got to bow out

Running Start
Was it in the heartbeat?
Was it from the footsteps?
With the beat of the music
The bleat of the battery
When the skins connected
There's a former me
There's a former you
Constantly, repetitively
Anticipating when you leave
And I don't know what I want
To work on these days
A ballad, a sonnet
A romantic dramedy or a play
It's all a different language
Transparent in the trunk
I wish I could feel it
Describe it
Pull the cork and let the oil spill out
Decipher it
Ultimate cluster of stars
Squeezed by embracing, loving arms
A similar blessing
Leaving me perplexed and guessing
Still walking with arrows in my back
Protecting what I had
Keeping in the blood
Waiting with bated breath
And with the cats

Brushing their bodies up against my shins
At least this way
With them
I can still feel soft and safe
Mesmerized by the lit lamps
Floating across the lake
Okay, I'm scared
But they're at least a good distraction
Along with the red sliver of sunrise
Between the mountains
Found in the thrift store painting
There's still a former me
There's still a former you
A swift cut that replaced the two

Melted Wolf
The crickets and cicadas
Are a little too loud for my eardrums
All the lemons and limes
Are far too sour for my taste buds
This is either a work of art
Or a warning sign
I've got cracked fingers
And a little time
From pushing daisies and picking papers
From the dirt and the inbox
A few reapers later and I'm indecisive
Monstrosity of stress and sacrifices
It's got a weird form
But it still looks familiar
At least the claws do
But even it agreed
These lemons and limes
Are too sour for the likes of me

Trip Twice

Is that plastic or water?
I can't tell
If it's crinkles or ripples
But then I hear the bell
Met someone who collects obituaries
As if they were baseball cards
Desperately trying to read in the dark
My life savings, gone
Thanks to arcade quarter eaters
Lucky I could even see
After years of staring at bright pixels
I still do with nostalgia and greed

And I'm going to stare at the sun next
Just a little while longer
Toads hissing at me
As I pass by, midnight in the dead of summer
They take me on and make me shatter
I wake up after what I guess is several days
Still some arrows in my ribcage

I've been a freak of nature
For far too long
Hidden beneath blue and gray fog
My shirts a little ripped
So is my skin
A few shadows undefined in a rumble
Am I in a fucking city or jungle?

Either one, I'm delighted
Short of breath and out of confinement
The joysticks broke
Fresh out of tokens, patience, and definitions
Leave and just be silent

Owls keep giving me the stink eye
In a prologue of autumn air
I hear them say, "Get a life!"
How the hell can they even speak?
I'm just pulling up scabs
And keeping tabs
On how it's been such an unproductive week

The Autumn Forge
Needle in the groove
Cockroach in the teeth
Sorry, I mean cocktail
Lots of alcohol to keep loose
Make sure to pull the strings straight
I'll make sure to leave your bones on the boat
At the tail end of the day
Static on every channel in my head
While I tally all my tattered clothes
Sprawled out on the floor and bed
Becoming like the others
The forgettable background characters
Being reeled in as irrelevant statistics
We just don't get paid enough
But the tasks and expectations
Keep piling up in a picture perfect pitcher
Overflowing on the counter
Until it tips over or cracks
And spills us out onto the floor
It's where I was last year
When I knew the diagnosis
Would be worse than what I thought before
And every night is just a new dimension
With different style, tiled floors
A mouth floating in suspension
Within 30 seconds my eyes are taken away
Worked out as a fear but mostly a favor
Less I'll have to see of a nightmare

Fear, All The Time

I've sworn that I don't have a sword to offer
I tried to forge it completely
Had my mouth sealed over with a symphony
Getting another pale chance
To protect with my dry hands
It's in the air and it's on the pad
I found truth and I found you
Slapping refrigerator magnets on the moon
I tripped over the cards you laid out
If it was a good reading, I'm sure I ruined it
Becoming hysterical and laughing through my teeth
Since I'm nowhere near the life I've wanted to lead

New House
Hungover at the deep end
Waking up
With quirks barely working

30 minutes later
I start to doze off
Eventually
These plans will get better

Legs crossed
While you sleep
Feigning security and certainty

Overestimating
Both charm and wits
Starving in the quiet
Good faith in a tonic
That's more than hard to swallow

I don't think
That you're a protector
You're barely familiar
With the fiction you've been fed

Long-standing
Don't feel bad
Every old phone book
Is becoming the newest fossil
Better than becoming
A rabid dog looking to tussle
Foaming furiously and confused
After all the spilled coffee
The pages are finally getting dried
From being left on discarded concrete
Tanning in the sunshine
Without a concern
And without a few pages
Let's just pretend
It's enjoying the sound of ambiance
Of steady and heavy traffic
Of pedestrians with a music echo
From their tongues and headphones
Some of those names and digits
At this point, may be long gone
But at least with this
They're remembered
Immortalized by someone

2 Augusts
Funeral parlors at the edge of the earth
2 Augusts have passed
And it still feels like the first
I still replay the gasp
The gurgle then the dreaded silence
I'd like to think I've found acceptance
Even since the other burial 10 years prior
I've been singing tunes
Of turnbuckles and tombs
Lionhearted but lethargic
Spinal fluid freezing over
Sparring partners showing pity & cowardice
A weekly workout of doldrums
I paid a pretty penny, a good sum
For standard situations
That lacked continuity and solutions
Dish towels with cardinals printed on them
I'm glad they bring mom some solace
And dad, I just can't describe it
There hasn't been any drop of waterworks
Just panic attacks when I recount it
But at least we're surviving
In the simplest of concepts

Slippers
Voice is just getting weak and lower
Syllables becoming an exercise
Sentences are cardio as you get older
Tired of the tide
Fishing out cigarette butts
From every green, black, & orange ashtray
Lighting, tasting them until the bitter end
Shivering while savoring the nicotine breath
Sitting on a scarecrow's throne
Sucking up all the water
It's so surreal and prone
To both failure and success
Crystal clear vinyl records spinning
Shouting at you to pass the time
It's hardly award winning
But this will do just fine
Bad timing for a breakneck pace
There's got to be someone on the balcony
Watching this whole story
Enjoying every detail they see

Invites
Leave out the crumbs
Keep us satisfied
And dangerous
In the ditch
With other diehards
Care and craft
Left in broken hands
Front to back adaptation
To new abilities
And frustrations

Buzz saw
Ball-peen hammer
Making a pine box for later
Masks and helmets
For the major
Boarding up windows
To keep safe from
Snake oil salesmen
No one has a cure
No one has a plan

Looking at reviews
The hum of parked cars
Brings some good news
A helpful fatigue
Dragged away in the breeze
Twirling strands of hair and heart

Snapping gum
At the quieter parts
Needed time and strength
To dance in the storm drains

Someone should knock
Before the house goes up in flames
Same for the birds
Coming down in a blaze
Balancing act with blame
Moths are upset
By just a few lights
Cold mountain dream
Resting on a forehead
Of a costume sold piece by piece

Need to buy something else
Books without thrills
And banter never ending
To distract from bills
That people keep sending
Pining after all complications
Push pins between
Each and every pore
Acupuncture antidote
Lightning shock to the core

No South

Can you crawl up the wall
Be the fly
Listen to them talk
Can you keep yourself hidden
From the judgment of cowardly men
That are driven to madness
Can you find any love or peace in the Northeast
Or do you cling to another pipe dream

The South had nothing
And you had nothing
Are you running
Or just simply drowning
You'll never reach that fortune or glory
Not now
Or ever in this story

Push the dirt on top of this
I don't care if it's a shallow grave
I don't care what you've wanted
You abandoned
You crushed
You let it fade

Worms

Lock hands with whoever you can
Hold tight
I'm sorry, I don't have a better plan
This will only hurt for second
When we hit the bottom of canyon

Pressured to pinch pennies
Attentions and intentions are never promising
Crafters complete their duties
Calm ripples in water
To crashing waves halfway through sailing
Does that seem less menacing?
Not really
I just feel like vomiting

Never more than you could support
Off with the heads of all the condors
To them, we're all food
They can't tell us apart
Rotting in the rain
An eyesore that causes pain
You're very bright and early

Leg Day

Ankles decided to slump over and quit on me
Good thing I was already being lazy
I should've known it was just the ghost
Trying to steal my legs again
They can straight up have them at this point
I'm not using them and too busy contemplating
Which bag of chips to pop open next
After a few laps around the foundation
Their sense of adventure is in for a rude awakening

Ceramic

It was the wrong growth
The wrong seed
The wrong path
Let lava and acid
Erupt from the chest and throat
It's a mask of weakness
Both putrid and bottomless
Smaller URLs in the eyes
In for such a sweet
Heartwarming surprise
Cutting fingers off
In a cathedral
A burning little cough
With every syllable

Apex
Funny how the bouquet
Sprouted from the rib cage
The colors are beautiful
But the petals are stiff
And there's not a single hint
Of aroma or calming bliss
This room may be warm
But the closet is a lot colder
Hide away in there to cool off a lot quicker
Felt the head snap back
And the spinal fluid spilled out
Drowning discarded price tags
Candle sticks at the base
Of a rusted cemetery gate
Taste buds tricked into thinking
It was pure sugar
When it was really craft glitter
Now a choke artist willing to litter
Find feet stomping on a patio
Lost gods flattened under the sole
Between the putrid smell of brake dust
And severe, stagnant lack of accepting defeat
By continuously betting on red
When, every time, it lands on black

Weird Balance

Saw some grainy footage
And you felt a little gutted
Different definitions of love
Swimming in heads
But drowning in the windpipe
No air getting through
Huffing and stomping
Without a destination
Lofty, tall goals
Longer than the standard liner notes
Unbelievable and unreachable
Better than being in a bind
But you hold a grudge to others
And their daily grind
Just for trying to keep you sublime
Told tales of delirious, demented management
Go ahead and kill it this December
The debts, the guilt trips
And maybe take back some tips
Don't seem to have favorite words
Looking for a gravy train
On airport runways
New and hackneyed lists
Are even harder to pitch
Pick the fruit, pick a plan
Rot with all you dream to loot
Let the graphite and ink streak
Get off your back and get off your knees

Status
Shovel: ready

Figures of speech: sheathed

Nerves: ripped off

Fears: fully blossomed

Conditions: pending

Mind: maladjusted

Timeline: short enough

Holes
Down turned blinds
And I'm lying in bed
Peaking through
Looking at the sky
And passing giants
While on my back
Feeling my tooth
Is loose again
I need a splint
To heal and fix
Maybe it'd be better
Using elbow grease
And some cement
I need to sing again
So it doesn't come out as
A hollow hallelujah to
Another shallow new year
For us to get through
I know there's much more
To both endure and explore
Doodling to pass the time
Putting anesthesia
In every single line
I used to want
The pictures to move
I used to love
The completed product
First the colors left

Then the ink
For a few years
Just remained a sketch
I guess I could sit up
Open the blinds
For clearer entertainment
But I'm not fortunate
Or known
To be very observant
Missed a few rounds
Between the giants
Thrown fists
Glass jaws
And grunting sounds
Guess I'll switch it up
Painting for now
Tried some acrylic
Then went to oils
Unsatisfactory results
And my appetite's spoiled
Maybe film a flick
 In watercolors and sticks
Macaroni art
This is a mess
And gruesomely poetic
Pulled the blinds up
Nothing but trees
The giants have left

Oils

It's okay to be afraid
To think tomorrow's going to be
Another wound to bandage
During a 15 minute break
It's dust in the wind
Pain under the peeling skin
Distorted and boring monsters
Sipping cheap gin

Two time bombs
Sitting comfortably in each palm
Fuses constantly hissing
You're just sweating on and on
You never signed up
For this sequence of snake eye rolls
Cheap t-shirts and war spoils
Of cracked and empty mugs

Writing 3 adventures from home
While the coral turns to stone
It'd be nice to be out at sea
But it's better to rest your knees
Learning a lesson
From your splitting fingerprints
That, your mind, and other aching bones
Are all going to be on the mend

Garland

Beat me over the head with bad news
Blueprints with calluses
And 2mm bolts and screws
I can taste the apathy in this apple
The empathy in this elixir
It took three hours but the shower
Is finally getting hotter
Looking for holiday feelings on tap
To wash certain words out of my hair
Cause I'm getting sick of the stare
That ignites in some eyes
When I emerge from a cave
As some sort of crazed vigilante in disguise
It's grown so old, so fast
A snow globe I can only crack
I was trying to break it
And free the village scene inside
Fearing the residents would drown
Fearing they wouldn't make it

Tan
You know in our down time
We're just fiddling around
With cluttered dreams

Just laying, baking in the sun
Saying you're going to build something better
But your tan is just getting redder

Decided to stick with the grass
And pass up the mattress
It's not the same shred of happiness

It takes a lot of nerve
To want this shrill summer to end
It's been a lot of work

We threw up the ink
And wrote down the words
While statues paraded on steps

Caught a couple wolves
Kicking, spinning, spitting, thrashing
With rats in the traffic

Curbside
Put my shopping list
On a piece of paper
Stained by nature
Twitching from the migraine
I've been suffering
In the breakdown lane

Sensory overload
From every car horn note
A rotten joke between my ears
I don't feel the least bit comical
Tone-deaf, half-hearted cheers
My sighs seem a bit livelier and vocal

Vanilla streaks across the sky
A couple claps of thunder
And my teeth are starting to grind
This sure as hell isn't fun
It's certainly not appealing
I'd rather be sleeping
Then be on another grocery run

Sew
Drinking and smoking
In a wax museum
For the better part of a decade
Let it all melt
I don't want the figures to have faces
The sun isn't good with conversations
Greasing palms on mini vacations
Just so I can breathe a little more comfortably

Keep notice of your simple things
Bleak, black claws
Ready to strike from the peripheral
You've burned 4 bridges
So just keep strolling
Enjoying the sight of lazy cardinals
Derrieres on dead branches

Who's to say
They're former family members
Or just a coincidence this winter
These same people won't let me be
They won't let me sleep
Managed to keep the mountain whole
But tore apart the galaxy

Small portions made
For so called holidays
Sharing didn't bring a single smile

That's expected when you can't cook for shit
I've barely mastered the microwave
Trying to patch together knowledge
With a hand me down sewing kit
Knees sort of shook for 2 seconds
All I did was stand still and crumble
I'll try to fix that too

Crabgrass
Right hook to the cheek
From karma and a dream catcher
Post it note reminders
Of the haircuts we've been skipping
Teeth are just chipping
Accidentally swallow like it's a snack
North and East streets to our backs
I guess that's better than swallowing wasps
And putting all the trust into a watch
In a classic move the stomachs turned
Going out for air, it burned
Character customization
And a smartphone chain letter
Is part of the blame plot
I'd like to see you do better
A nervous thread
A courier with a loose breath
Crashed down on a Tuesday
Until we found someone to save
The sermon was just gibberish
The candles weren't even lit
Speaking to the sun like it's a nervous twitch
Tiny pieces of talons make a nice collection
Better than the glass bottles of sand
We got from the same beach
Or the flowers we stole from the land
The timing's kind of impeccable
The messages will remain inaudible

Price and Note
Spent your money on pens
And paltry attention
It's a small race
A small taste
Coin purse winnings
Intangible as
Imaginary friends
And ghosts
We shook hands with
In the past

Mentioned

I sure wouldn't mind
Getting drunk off of dandelion wine
For the rest of my days
In a saline solution haze
That cleaned out my eyes
From looking at pollution
And presenting ideas that aren't bright
Piece by tiny piece
And a little bit of cheap paste
I got a bigger taste
Of trying to fix
What wasn't even broken
I know I don't sound enthusiastic
But there's no need for you to panic
These irregularities
Happen quite often and normally
In and out of the blue
And sometimes shades of pink and charcoal
Someone suggested other colors
To up the showmanship
I'm fine with the routine
And sort of want to quit
I'll brush up and get ready
For the road to swallow us whole
I won't even kick and scream
It's going to be the easiest way
To finally hibernate
When I wake up

After a few weeks
Or maybe a few months
I'll be sorry for the sour morning breath
At least it doesn't smell like death
I'm just trying to forget the history
Erase my own head
But mostly want a good night's sleep

Sticks

This tree has bloody roots
We grew worried when it started to pool
But there are barely any rings
That's why we sing the songs we sing
Meager, mild, and without any hint of style

We're growing ever more worried
That we're in denial
Blended haphazardly but blended together
Accept it graciously while enjoying the weather

Watered down in this awakening
Shouted out while firmly yet falsely grinning
The clouds are different colors now
Storms are coming without an ounce of sound

Did you want a subtle scenery
Or something that came to life briefly?
I could propose these questions until I gasp
I just want to give you something I know will last

Usual Habits
Day to day calendars
Of lilies and lilacs
Going over pamphlets
Of how to practice better habits
Still not used to the shift
From snowy reception
To slow buffering
I guess it's to get study groups
To finally pay attention
Instead of falling flat
And going numb
Stop searching
Begin rehearsing
How to rob the bank
Then walk the plank
One more stiff drink
Before we sank
Knowing these adventures
Never even took place

Giant Day

Integrated and interrogated
Blood in the hair
And calmly negotiated
Boxed up and simply stagnant
Playing parts with a deadpan stare
In every choir and pageant
I tried to shout out
From a lack of patience
Knowing I can't replace this
Needing to be famous
The curves on the road
This spine made feverishly
With steel and stone
I'll just let terrifying shapes
Slap some sense into me
Producing dents on the cheeks
A chill wracked my body
When the teeth were at my throat
And there's a new ship coming in
With grey hairs and gambling problems

Barrel
Shoved in the back pocket
Folded behind an expired credit card
Left to rot in a wallet
The limp reminders
Of all the joyous disasters
That you danced through
That panicked you
Left you singing in the shower
And biting your nails
Nuanced nightmares
Of stealing railroad tracks
Weeping from generosity
And losing what you never had

On The Keep
Living to be thirsty
In the corner of the cage
Trying to earn pennies
Betting spectators
That they can't guess my age
It's the only thing I can think of
Since I keep adding to the sink
Dirty dishes and laundry tend to pile up
I wrote a novel
And left it all in the stein
When it's usually meant
For dark beer and boxed wine
Clean up the band aids
And find us the proper change
Burnt the roof of my mouth
On peppermint and pocket lint
For different and difficult occasions
Tailor-made for confusion
The grease starts to hit the statues
Then peace between the dog and vacuum
Seeing through closed eyes
And coupon clippings
Why did I cling to the same system?
The same outdated settings?

Magic

Go back to reading all these books
To the beat of certain songs
Then a silent alarm chimed in
Left you thinking and dreaming
The best way to dive into the moon
Is aim for the reflection in the lake
Bringing such a shockwave
That the ripples echo past your entry
Making the stars wobble and shake

Pigeons
Okay
I know I don't have a concrete update
Pissing in the garden
Turning heads when I leave and won't explain

Revenue
Made from a paltry amount of views
Figured out the burden
When I recklessly weave through the news

I swig
Take a drink while everyone would dig
Too much to share
Only treasure that was buried were trash and twigs

Cement
Poured through my throat to keep my lament
Being a statue without care
New home for pigeons to sit and repent

Nonsensical
A couple old souls
With palaces and thrones
Tastes of apple and cinnamon
In every liquid

Smoke and pen
Building skeletons
A pregnant pause
Dropping jaws
It's a standard silence
For whoever's driving
Bending book spines
And leaving crease lines

Symmetry in a cemetery
Paper and charcoal over the grave
Scribbling to get
The designs and the name
Unfamiliar and furious
Comical and serious
While staring at the glow
On the lens and chrome

Could've used
Just a staggering few
Lullabies and screams
To help with the scene

Order Up

Is it even a sea
Or is this debris?
Should I be floating on my back or stomach
Or curled up and sinking several feet?
Digging my nails into my knees
No matter the position
It's a fair escape
But it'll get old later on in the day
Kind of relaxing
More so terrifying
Because I swear I overheard
Sharks are keeping their teeth sharpened
Licking their lips
Bringing salt and garlic
And I'm just being melancholy & oblivious
Eat up, enjoy your meal with no effort
You deserve it

Current & Coal
Born in a mine
Since they didn't want me to know
The true colors of the sky
Coughing up coal and blood
Until I reached 29
Dug a way out and grew feathers
Flying was fleeting
A quick outcome of failure
I guess the important result
Was finally identifying the sky
Blue, green, gray and white
Then by some miracle
I decided to go blind
Making do with what I just saw
It was brief
But the mind took snapshots
And the imagination altered them even more
Regardless of the time or mood
It never became a bore

Burning Liquid
You were right
This isn't quite
The home for my head
It's a blight
I could find
Better days
Paralyzed in a frame
It's not like
I'm drinking fire
Anymore while
Hitting the spike
In my fever
The rush will
Soon expire
It's a good haste
And I certainly prefer
The awful taste

Litter
Discarded switchblade
By Silver Lake
Found while scuffing up the trail
In slippers and grogginess
And a tablespoon of sheer will
Just hoping you were home
While I was spacing out at the stream
It was a gorgeous scene
With me being the only blemish
Running scared and on weak steam
Or probably stale cereal
And lame levels of caffeine
Picking up the litter can't wait
Even though I'm half awake

Nautical

We're not moving again
We're not shaking our heads
Leaving the liquor and wine
In their respectful cabinets
There's something else worth drinking
Getting drunk on nostalgia and wishful thinking

Nibbling on normalcy
Chuckling like it's a delicacy
Swearing on sobriety
As soon as we reach a new shore
I'm going to catch a quick snooze
Apologies in advance for hogging the booze
And especially if I snore

After a few more gulps
Fingers crossed at the hull
While the current carries us out
Some new discoveries to make
And some new people to let down

Pop

Tears, gasps, and chokes
On beat with the beeps
From the hospital machines
Trying to escape
To the outskirts of my brain
An unkempt garden
Where none of this was happening
The short breaths
The blue sheets
Became unruly vines
And beautifully chaotic weeds
Below the arches of my feet
Gobs of paint on the trees
It's a subpar escape from reality
I may have peeled my mind away
But the eyes are a different story
All I can say now is sorry
For missing your send off
Because I was being selfish
And trying to escape

Effort & Venom
That pain fell right through the flesh
I ignored another mess
I gained another stain
Now I'm sitting in the park
Avoiding poison darts
Shot with piss poor aim
Retreat back home to start sketches
Of snakes in the basement
I just find the line work
Calming and intricate
As the camera panned out
My hands and mind started to jerk
After the seclusion, it hit
The drawings came to life and bit
I can't keep clear
Or remotely calm anymore
I'm getting dizzy with fear
Trying to keep my footing
Keeping my body
From receding to the floor

Overlapping Dialogue

I keep trying and trying but it became a bit daunting
I know the lack of sleep is my own fault
But your projections are even more haunting
Can you even call it help after this?
Anchors down on both my wrists
Using my palms as a canvas
Sour smiles and meager predictions
I just order the usual
Humming out the horrors
Ignoring their wake and funeral
I fell out of the chair due to poor balance
But I'm still certainly on the wagon
I'm still beating off the branches
You shook from the trees
That kept weighing down my shoulders
And buckling my knees
All brought on by a partial pettiness
And severe lack of finesse
I felt starved then stewed
Tasting gamey and crude
Be honest, it's nothing new
Cooking up the trouble was cathartic
Been pretending to pull
A treasure along the shore
The sword grew dull as you grew bored
Good luck at either the Atlantic or Pacific
I know one thing's for certain
We're both going to need it

Self Sufficient

An interesting game
With folding mirrors and timepieces
Being eaten alive
By thoughts of nirvana and utopia

These are all just the same notes
On a typical day
Gold in the gravel
And a not-so-subtle eye roll

Busy staring at wounds
Trying to etch in a few simple tattoos
Around them and the infection
It stings from the attention

Good project before the trip
Enjoying the buzz from panic
That set in from the ruse
As I lost my pulse from sabotage

I'm not building a church
Or burning a bridge
How can I manage either
When I can barely make breakfast?

Divulge
Growing old
And wanting out
College ruled paper
Pencil shavings
Inspiration
3 good ingredients
In a recipe
With a little less doubt
Than an unread note
Empty coatroom
And the image
Of someone blowing smoke

Porcupines
It's all just waning
In my mind, in the sky
And in the grave
Others are buying bullshit by the pound
They can't devise a solid reason
At least it's quiet 6 feet in the ground
Intro & intermission chapters
Permanent scars
And discarded candy wrappers
Rotting the teeth that are speaking names
They want to keep above the sun
Lucky to be in 7th place
Banging pots and pans together for fun

Taking naps in the middle of battles
Miscalculations made
While stamping out marigolds
And considering the last few weeks
Are we sure it's springtime?
Early birds have been picking up dead worms
With chipped and broken beaks
Impacted teeth are finally being extracted
It might be a slow process
Of healing, but we've earned it
Such a fate, such a shake
To the spine and the discs
Cartilage climbs up the ladder
It is a new and will be a better age

Thermal

My sleep and snores swelling up each night
Like my throat and fiery sinuses
Running away from the medicine

Someone's been burning down a field
At the climax of my bizarre nightmare
Antagonists cackling and they won't even yield

Hitting myself with a mallet
To make up for lost time
Collapsed below some sort of archway
Holding hands with an unknown name

I can't even make out the rest of the scenes
It's a constant state of being eaten alive
By peers, strangers, and other workers in the hive

Fads In The Air

Counterfeit conscience
Popping every joint
With improper precision
Tongue pinched between teeth
Catalog of comedically timed
Wilhelm screams
Another view quietly skewed
And quickly deteriorating
Walking on quicksand
And quickly becoming ill
Depleted after taking a spill
Happily I'll sink
Haphazardly leaving
The universe on my sleeve
And scrapes on my skin
It's going to sting
It's going to make me tremble
Wear a mask and practice magic
For precautionary measures
Reaching one too many chapters
I want stuttering doubt
Car alarms going off
Causing me to go crazy
Muscles growing lazy
Used band aid on a broken bone
A pick me up from comfort food
Seems empty calories
Are becoming the best company

Color In Color
A smile stiffening everyday
In brief playlists
And worthless blueprints
Pacing the room
Lacing ideas through a tomb
Glowing pale in the cheeks
Green in the eyes
And red in the teeth
Because I've been rifling
Through old photos and files
That could go on for miles
While the sun cracked
Injuring off the gray
Through the clouds
Making it bleed orange and violet
It was so refreshing and loud

Lectures
New coat of paint on the barn doors
Sweet precision of cigarette burns
Designer's choice with insect carcasses
And various crumbs on the floor
Noticing a couple of half-assed tantrums
And regrettable purchases

An empty promise of going West
Inside this little lecture hall
What's going to be left behind?
Unheard apologies that weren't worth the time
With zero need to be revived

Blood blisters scabbing beneath
Each and every fingernail
Is better than feeling this weak
And how this will linger and fail
Trying desperately to recall
If it even started out strong or not

But it's a busted schedule
Between all the memoirs and mixtapes
Waving a wand that was misplaced
Across the sea in a bottle
There isn't even a skeleton crew
Working inside this skull

But the wheels are somehow turning

Utensils and tools clanging on the ground
Forever dazed and dull
They fit in with the beer cans and flowers
Ran passed during a graveyard jog
Too bad the legs are broken
Now at the mercy of junkyard dogs

Bells On Sunday

I can definitely carry on
This wasn't a necessary linchpin
Or a catchy song
It was a root canal and sting
And illusion in
Improvising on a hill
I don't react at all
Just swallow a few paper pills
Granite fences
Bordering the cemeteries
Recalling Sunday mornings
With the scent of blueberries
Little lost luxury
Pacing the following Mondays
When I wasn't even awake
Until the cartoon marathons
A childhood caffeine
The only thing that got me up

Catalogs
Carefully crafted notes
On a typical day
The last calm weekend
Keying lines
In the racing stripes
I noticed the rotting at the bottom
For nearly 2 years
Now alive and trying to dance
To sing and sync to the sound
Using a novelty hammer
To hit a hollow crown
Storytimes and lullabies
Put out with a few stammers
Blisters and calluses in the background
Pulling leaves off the trees
Before they chickened out
Naturally from the winter sneeze
Pulsating pain
Inside the mask and makeup
But perfectly fine with the pacing
Humidity letting pages curl
Here's something major that was missed
Clear signs of danger
Of a spine with a split
And there are different compilations
To keep us all company
While carefully grasping
Paper handles on a coffin

Sleeper

A bitter animation
With more complications
Than I can count
On both hands
Motion lines
To signify
Discomfort
And shaking in the shelter

A day before
I helped you hunt down
Treasures from myth and lore
And truth from songs
Trending
Like tithings in a tree
Ready to feed

Tear ducts
Revving up
Bad habits
Disappearing
6 miles into the sky
Yellow traffic signals
Blinking through
These shades
Morse code on the wall
From the window

Different phases
Through a fisheye lens
A suit accompanying
The wrinkles
In the cheeks
From the fake smile
But it's unseen
Attention to detail
And drumming

Late Night Vision

Dining alone near canvas and charcoal
Pulling at my own set of strings now
But I don't have a license to drive this thing

Scraps and sediment where I lay down
After trying to get into the ring
A ballet of clumsiness through the ropes

Either pacing or paralyzed by a payphone
Rings left by beer cans and condensation
Stains getting burnt into concrete and stone

Still letting out laughs from the lungs
Couldn't even find a crumb
To taste or even choke on

There's a couple of receipts and sleeves
Rolled up and ready for the ink stains
Exploding from pens and phantom pains

Demographic

While it felt like a long year
It went fairly quick
Sculpting my own skin
And not getting sick
Slowly connected
Through coin collections
Destructive daily routines
And spiral staircase dreams

Trying to press pause
But we'll settle for slow motion
Starting with a hiss and a hiccup
Catacombs filled to the brim
Another October
Thriving on reruns and leftovers
This sitcom is a riot
And now my skin is peeling
Rotting out like a usual 30 something

Crows

Just wait until
Tomorrow spills
Begging for this venom
This ferocity, this vicious
And vocal delivery
A nuisance with a new look
Black feathers
And a few fake books
I guess in the long run
The lectures did nothing
But make these lips fall off
Replaced with plastic
Glass and aluminum
It's either off to the races
Or off to the bed
It ends up being neither
Unsure of what's next
We thought we heard
A recognizable chime
But it was just you swimming
With the music
Getting farther out and distant
Napping through the humidity
Thought of creating
With clipart and construction paper
Strange dreams cemented in the walls
And in a small corner of it all
Artificial flowers

Being planted in a garden
Somehow the stems
Prove to be growers
Just like the two
Distinct sunset views
And the cold air
We felt coming from the fire
Along with the books
Came some fake feathers
Made from string and leather
So they're complete
Sad stories without a structure
No middle or end
Barely even a beginning
Caution tape at the center
And discomfort in the deep end
Breathing the same cold fire
Traipsing through muck and mire
Feeling naked
Even with the masks
Hiding signs of aging
Baked deep in the crust
Next to a flurry rush
Of panic and pampering
Equal amounts of yammering
Horror stories hitting us
In one fell swoop
Is it going to rain or what?

Won't Be Missed
Another night of rotting
In our own subpar art
Recruiting regrets
With hints of working hard

Pulling a plastic thread
From a crack in the skull
Watch it unravel

The ground kept moving
Not shaking but skittering
Fire ants at the feet
And I'm shivering

Aimed and projected
In a different direction
Poorly drawn bullseye
For all the spit

Keep It Down
Stuck in a garage
Trying to fix a bike
That I can't even ride
Pining to have conversations
With September skies

Character with comedic paranoia
Showing from the time dinner starts
Until we're well past dark

Rare negatives
With sharp and mild smiles
Scraping stones on the window
Of an abandoned hospital

Maybe a minor measure
Of a stone garden we couldn't hope to save
Even if we had the pleasure
We're not miracle workers

A sting a minute
As we stare at the sun
Until we blackout
Not every day can be a fantasy
But it helps in some instances
Especially when nights are sleepless

Chimes
If it's all the same to you
I won't favor the fiction this time
There's a better flavor
And fitting in truth and how it chimes
Where the ice in the driveway
Is still making a fool of me
And back aches that went on for more than a day
Made me accept the lack of invincibility
There are tools in every room
And I can't fix a thing
I'm sick of stretching in unhealthy ways
To make certain victory bells ring

Toned

There's only a couple
Oil paintings
And figure drawings
From the past
Let them rot
In the closet
For a span
Of time that flew by
Posters that faded
And bleached
In the sun
Edges frayed
Corners curled up
Running down
To do the dishes
In a gaudy kitchen
With decorative
Scuffed wood paneling
Some left sinking
And shrinking
With the soap
Chisel away
Like it's stone

Spring Motivation
A few unique birch trees
And building blocks
For make believe
A stone fence with padlocks
Fingerprints
Pushing in a sense
Under some guidance
Flower petals
Just as strong as stone
Used to lift and live alone
Yanking on their own roots
Sincerely insisting
They can handle the weight
Take a break
Take a load off
Kick your roots up
Sigh and snooze
In relief
It's in good hands now
Leave the rest to me

Like A Bull
It's just a soundtrack
Sticking to me like glue
Certain hues in the folds
Cathartic composure in the notes
So it's a little faded
Like paper blueprints
Frayed and dilapidated
But still has the same effect
It's like a type of poison
Tricking its way into the my lungs
Swishing around in my gut
Part of my brain
Replaying your last few days
Your last few breaths
The balloons popped
I stumbled between
Flowers both wilted and chopped
Behind a few of my uncles
And pallbearer gloves that barely fit
I could feel the spasm in muscles
After we lifted you in the back
My entire body in a daze
I couldn't find a place to stare
It felt like a thousand years
Just passed around me
I accepted it
But it still wasn't fair

Galaxies
Two spills
Running through the ink
And having a chitchat

The sunlight
Biting into the blinds
Trying to tell a backstory

What was the reason
That kept this heart from beating
And counting stones in the ceiling

Drawing constellations
On the walls with crayons
Quickly becoming elaborate creations

Shooting a name
Through that galaxy of paraffin wax
And drywall that won't last

Copper Vines
Pushing words
Out of my mouth
After alcohol
Rolled down the throat
Steamroller tongue falling out
Syllables broken and starting to float
When I'm falling in
I'm a fidgeting fugitive
The caffeine kept me
From sitting still
I couldn't find a place to live
And let my thoughts fill
The entire room
And flood out
It comes and it goes
The poetry and the prose
Just like the bruises
The purple and blue
On the knees and elbows
Shapeshifting as they heal
Pain shrinking as part of the deal
But still lingering in the mind
Causing a recoil
Or maybe a flinch
Quickly filling up
On screenshots of the turbulence
The pressure coiling around
Constricting like a snake

There's not much air at stake
The same old mess
Taking root and growing
Branching out
Avoiding
Obstacles and damages
That would have
Halted all its progress
Copper vines around my frame
But I've adapted
To the new process
The day to day

Healing Weather
Split the seams and the seasons
Repair it with some stronger thread
These are the type of days
Where rain won't rinse away
Any type of unplanned pain
Pulling up grass to pass the time
Stomping on leaves enjoying the crinkle and colors
Throwing snow at satellites
Using the summer sun as a crutch
All this weather throughout the year
Was just enough

Spring Forward
A commercial break
Paid for by pocket change
Mind picked clean
Of old wounds & anxieties
Feasting on fiction
Like I was paid to do it
Calloused hands
Tearing off calendar pages
I'm a little out of it today
And will be for several more
Since some folks had daylight to save
Shuffling feet through salt and slush
Unable to wake up
Lifting fear and fog
With my bare hands
Using bloodshot eyes
To drill through a mountain
Forgetting the fiction
I just gorged on
I'll admit
My gut was greedy
Instead focusing
On the lucid dream
I had inside of a picture frame
Blowing off some steam
Shaking away the shivers
I've felt in my bones
From the ice and snow

Tide

I left a nervous shipwreck
With scraped knees
By the skin of my teeth
And I appear to be queasy
Wheezy with baggy eyes
Sloppy handwriting
Under the typography
Drawings resembling sea monsters
On napkins and school desks
Terrorizing the ship's crew
They're all choking on the thick smoke
Activating a gagging reflex
Swallowing metaphors and sick jokes
I got out as the smoke hit
Rinsed out my lungs with saltwater
Pounding on the shore
An imprint of my fist
Cooked into the sand
But I coughed so much that
My vision went black like asphalt
Eyelids tightened and sealed shut
Then my lungs close like a vault
Sprang up awake and surprised
Clawing at the sky
Seagulls laughing when I came to
Though I'm a bit dazed and confused
I need to brush off
Stroll on and continue on like the tide

Used To It
Well rested from the insomnia
Healthy and spry from all the sugar
Unscathed and not a scratch
From all the thrill seeking
I found in a car crash
Feeling cooled off from the fever
Shivering comfortably from the heat
Breathing is steady while drowning in the deep
Walking just fine after the fall
Legs are just bending a different way, that's all
Twisted and split thumbs
Up in the middle of the night
A quick review to show that I'm doing just fine

New Tastes
We need something to get us through
Bottle of red or white
Lager, stout or ale
Anything goes as long as we mix
Our feelings in just right

Peppering paranoia
Over this entire conversation
Seasoning my usual distrust
For more of a kick to the tongue
Give me some gasoline and caffeine
I'm just biting my lips for bloodlust

It tastes like a timebomb
Soot rolling across my tastebuds
Pricking like needles from a cactus
Sediment slowly tumbled down my throat
I'm punching upwards
Choking, reeling from the smoke

Too many syllables
Plucked from the trees
Tasting as stale and dry
As the air in my backyard or out at sea

Lucid

Suffering an allergic reaction
It was a strange condition
Asking for advice and permission
From someone nonexistent
I'd rather be distant than persistent
In certain aspects
No, I'm not jealous
Just banging a hammer on a callus
And if this is just a dream
Then hear me out until you wake up
I've got fake feathers but they're quite tough
Getting me airborne through the stormfront
I can at least admit this was fun

Stamps

Parents didn't raise a worrier
But it sure seems that way
Certainly not a warrior of any kind
No shield, sword or any sort of weaponry
Just butterfly bandages
A forged narrative
Scraped elbows and knees
To appeal to the crowd
Lips quivering from the stage
The pain and body shakes
Nothing is even that loud right now
The grenades and screams
All a dull whisper across the scenery
Courage stripped from fingertips
Picking at the bricks
Frantically moving the rubble
Panicking while I move the stones
Then dancing alone
Watching a fire from up high
A lot of rot between my palms
I keep the pulled pins in my pockets
The blast from that hit faster and harder
Than the smell of sweet rockets
Despite all that I'm still standing
That's got to count for something

Scruff
A few minutes make all the difference
A memory makes my smile seem twisted
Nonexistent eyes keep staring
Burning holes through my neck
Losing my balance and bearings

The bristles from the broom
Sweep up the last few measly crumbs
I don't even remember what I took back
But I remember there's no room

All the times I try to forget
Are tethered and chained to my brainstem
Scouring and scrubbing it off
With no luck
It's still present

Left tagged out in the rain
Cataloging what I can
Frightened by the vast size
Of the sea and starry skies

It's time versus me
I know I won't win
Since I'm barely even swinging
Sat there and stared
Watching me collect dust

Epitaphs

Measuring mishaps and mistakes
With branches I found on the path
Tripped over every manic landmine
Twisting my ankles like it was part of the plan
Standing up straight
Then finding glory in the gutter
Pigeon toed as the engine sputters
Small drop of gas to keep me going
I try to take a quick photo
Of the mountain range
And writing a new motto
It's been a decade with very few epitaphs
That I had to chisel in my memory banks
Not of loved ones or celebrities
Not even favorite characters
That authors killed off to spite the readers
This mausoleum is just filled with memories

Eraser Shavings

So what's essential to the sketch?
Cleaner lines and colors?
Some shading or erasing?
Can't remember how the paper
Felt against the skin
Just been smudging the charcoal and ink
Staining the scenery
And ruining the details

Bold outlines
And unrefined brushstrokes
Sharp reds and yellows
For the backgrounds and traffic lights
For the cityscape and signs
To give a better a direction
I've just been taking random turns
Throwing occasional hand signals
Spicing things up
With trial, error, and tribulations

I've sharpened the pencils
And wet the brush
Far too much
Haven't been wiping the slate clean
It's just layer after layer
Of new and mixed media
Still life, object, flora, fauna or scenery
Portraits and figure drawings

Are out of the question
I couldn't draw hands if my life depended on it

Maybe this time
I'll actually erase and start over
It's going to take a while
To figure out what to create next
I'm sure I'll be perplexed
And still circle back
Wondering what happened to the old ideas
And creative process

Second Nature

You felt it
The deafening silence
The weight of it
Wood splitting between the ears
Sprouting through the drums
With silverweed and fungus
It's a new decoration
Rather than a new direction
Movements designed around the music
You don't try to hide it
Breathing deeper than ever
Because you have long lungs to fill up
Letting out the loudest scream
That you can muster
A benchmark for the bucket list
Reading up on a different afterlife
As if you have the time
But the dagger missed
You've still got a few minutes
To socialize and get high
On taking all the credit
Of what was carved in the bark
But you just lay in a cavern
Enjoying the feel
Of the cold dirt of the earth

The Party
Water droplets on my fingertips
Pocket knife to flick them off
A silly motive
To carve a motif
Along the fingerprints
My name might stand for "crown"
Nowhere near being a prince
I celebrate the same way
As everyone else
Cold shoulders in the corner
With lukewarm bottles of alcohol
But my hands have frostbite
I can't feel my toes either
Looks like it's going to be a long night
I kept the time capsule
Buried below the campfire
I only made it through one sunset
Before I dug it back up
I just wanted to feel the rush
The joy and sadness from nostalgia
A melancholy meanderer
With a brand new shovel
I've already used twice
At least the breeze out here is nice

Fences
Keep the kicks coming
Keep throwing punches
Don't let up even once

I'll admit there was a speed bump
A spike strip to blow the tires out
I miscalculated the jump

Found the fence could use fixing again
Think instead of sticks
I'll use bricks for a better defense

Steady clash
Between doom and gloom
Turned it into sawdust and ash

I couldn't fix it after
I'm just sitting in the dirt and rubble
With both hands glued together and laughter

Cedarwood

The smell of cedar invading this room
Wood wick crackling
But it won't burn out soon
Nailed to the floor while water washes through
There's still some space to breathe and burn
The door won't open
But the knob just keeps on spinning
The hinges trembling
At least it's not hazy in here anymore
No orange glow from the windows
Just imprints on the wallpaper
Of hands and faces
Lost throughout the years
They're all still here
Just like he scent of cedar
Still swaying strong

Wasps
Very strange story
Of fairy tale glory
Who's breathing down your neck?
Arch rival or arch nemesis?
Driving you to sprint into the bars
Looking for some liquid gold solace
Whatever you drank, burned
Like wasps down the throat
Pushing a shiver down your spine
Recalling it will make you wince
From time to time
For now, you don't mind
This is quickly becoming a stumbling waltz
Out to the sidewalk after last call
Frustrated in a tiny corner of the world
Trying to salvage your own work
Promising yourself that in the morning
You're going to do your best
Trust us, don't feel bad
Everyone has had
The same wretched crack through the chest

Thermos
AM hits
Caffeine, caffeine, caffeine
Put it in an IV drip
I was awake all the prior nights
And need more than a sip
PM hits
Espresso, espresso, espresso
That may be a shot too many
But the IV's dried up and empty
So I just don't know
Head scratching
Then crashing
Until I have herbal tea
To stir and swish
Every day, every second like this
Coffee until I crash after the twitch

The Lids
Confusion is key here for a while
Waking and waiting for a break in the style
With a twisted belly filled with corrupt files
Untangled, it would go on for miles

Jacked up prices in a certain market
It's a niche one and random at that
The kind of people who only find love in lockets
Polite, they may appear to be but only for a profit

The idiotic words came out unedited
Grammar and punctuation unchecked
Final dialogue, submitted verbatim
Back to patient zero with original symptoms

Once a day carried away
By the wind and waves
A wholesome but chaotic chain
A flowered tongue
And silver spoon to greet the days

Wrapped what you could around your fingers
Manila envelopes sealed by frugal strangers
Think twice when fulfilling favors
Gingerly realizing which feelings have bitter flavors

Simplified and staggering counterfeits
Of well-known and bitter tasting trysts

Reorder some new checks
Until the balance is different
This is a clear cut sign of a brand new section

Mythological

There's a basilisk in the brewery
Ruining, spilling all that the barrels hold
There's only a couple tears shed and seen
Only from a few who would be so bold
How heavy is the heart of each man?
Altogether, as much as a grain of sand
In both weight and worth
It's a circus clown & a card dealer's curse

Kind of like the bats in the belfry
But not nearly as damaging
It left a few souls lost at sea
And it traded a lot of blood for filthy money
If you're waiting for that behavior to stop
There's a better chance of the drunks
Cleaning up after themselves on the bar top

The tiger just gave you a boatload of lip
No sign of its teeth, it just wanted to share
"I just miss the whiskey!"
It yelled and several related instantly
Share a few quick coffees
A few cheap cigars
With self-hatred of your own species
And dying to escape to the stars

Slapstick
Felt a shock
Through the sole of my shoe
Sunburnt forearms
Right before I get a tattoo
Brain freeze
Behind the eyes
This is all feeling
A bit paranormal
The trips, falls, and spills
No skin peeling
No scrapes
Just bandages
And comedic timing

Grand
Bloodhound, be brave
Let your own name give you strength
Watch your master
Pluck every bead
From a rosary

The picture was perfect
But he was poorly persuaded
Offers a garment as a gift
But no one finds it impressive

Watching mountains explode
And burning down to your level
All of these theatrics
Are just paltry distractions
You aren't waiting on the world to cave in
You're just looking for someone to stay with

Everything Seems Louder

Palm readings on par with pocket lint
I didn't even flinch
Twisting my tongue
To clean my teeth and gums
Chasing my own tail
That I set on fire
While every consequence
Scratches at the door
It's time for a new dance
While I amplify an echo
I'm determined tonight
To start and win some kind of fight
But it'll probably be a flight response
I'm filming the full collapse
No directors or scripts
Complete improv and relapse
But there's a sudden and subtle silence
After dancing to wild years
But I still kept on floating
With the fire and the fears
I kept in this old house
They're sealed in different pockets
And separate walls
But they're still pretty loud
They've been exiled for a little while
I'm sure they're ready for the next round
Slanted sunrise and pale knuckles
Crashing through the spackle

Fluorescents flaring through
Tanning the skin
It never goes away
Steadily steaming for decades
Suddenly the VCR
Sprang back to life
Family movies flowing
Like background noise in the destruction
Finally, the grief catches up to me
Tear ducts understood the assignment
Fires extinguished
And I'm flooding the floor
Crawling on all fours
Laughing through it all
All of the lectures
All of the loss
All of the pain
It hurt but I'm alive
My chest doesn't feel as tight
To my feet, poised
Ready to rebuild
Door wide open for some new noise

Steve is an ordinary dude from the Berkshires. A lover of drawing, painting, thrifting, reading and collecting books. You can find his artwork over at https://www.instagram.com/montydrawz